# *If You Look Like Me*

S. A. POOLE

If You Look Like Me
Copyright © 2018 by Sha'rod Poole

All rights reserved. No part of this publication may be reproduced, distributed, or transmitted in any form or by any means, including photocopying, recording, or other electronic or mechanical methods, without the prior written permission of the author, except in the case of brief quotations embodied in critical reviews and certain other non-commercial uses permitted by copyright law.

Tellwell Talent
www.tellwell.ca

ISBN
978-0-2288-0505-2 (Paperback)
978-0-2288-0506-9 (eBook)

# Table of Contents

Chapter 1: The Beginning . . . . . . . . . . . . 1
Chapter 2: Wake Up. . . . . . . . . . . . . . . 11
Chapter 3: Balance . . . . . . . . . . . . . . . . 19
Chapter 4: Views and Values . . . . . . . . .27
Chapter 5: Wellness . . . . . . . . . . . . . . . 37
Chapter 6: Your Own Twos . . . . . . . . . . 47
Chapter 7: The Next Move. . . . . . . . . . .55
Chapter 8: Stand Tall . . . . . . . . . . . . . . .63
Chapter 9: Take It Easy . . . . . . . . . . . . . 71
Chapter 10: No Regrets . . . . . . . . . . . . .79

# Table of Contents

Chapter 1: The Beginning . . . . . . . . . . . . .1
Chapter 2: Wake Up. . . . . . . . . . . . . . . .11
Chapter 3: Balance. . . . . . . . . . . . . . . . .19
Chapter 4: Views and Values . . . . . . . . .27
Chapter 5: Wellness . . . . . . . . . . . . . . . .37
Chapter 6: Your Own Twos . . . . . . . . . .47
Chapter 7: The Next Move. . . . . . . . . . .55
Chapter 8: Stand Tall . . . . . . . . . . . . . . .63
Chapter 9: Take It Easy . . . . . . . . . . . . .71
Chapter 10: No Regrets . . . . . . . . . . . . .79

There's nothing more
important than
Being who you are the
way you see fit.
I want to inspire readers to strive
Above the surface,
dream beyond the
Stars and live in a peaceful world
that will inspire others to be aspiring
Themselves.

S.A. POOLE

## Chapter 1

# The Beginning

If You Look Like Me…you were conceived. Born like a baby bird hatching in a tree. A new edition to life, a seed with the potential to grow and become whatever you want to be.

If You Look Like Me…when you opened your eyes to see, someone smiled, someone cried, someone didn't even squeak. You yawned, you laughed, you got excited when it was time to eat. You had a long day, then someone said, "Sweet Dreams" before you fell asleep.

If You Look Like Me…you were conceived. Born like a baby bird hatching in a tree. A new edition to life, a seed with the potential to grow and become whatever you want to be.

If You Look Like Me…when you opened your eyes to see, someone smiled, someone cried, someone didn't even squeak. You yawned, you laughed, you got excited when it was time to eat. You had a long day, then someone said, "Sweet Dreams" before you fell asleep.

If You Look Like Me…you crawled, you rolled over, you took your first step, and you sat in your special seat. You learned how to talk, spell, write and read. You had a first day of school, made friends or just blankly stared and didn't speak.

If You Look Like Me…you had recess, lots of playing with other kids, shared lunchtime and heard the sound or felt the vibration of the class bell. You made your way across the stage even if you needed help or decided to do other things to find yourself.

If You Look Like Me…you once gave a speech, shook hands, waved at your classmates and accepted a sheet all rolled up nice and neat…or you were just an attendee, because some things you just don't achieve.

If You Look Like Me…you faced a new world with goals to complete. Things don't go as planned but, on the other hand, things aren't that bad. You feel like you've failed…strangers may give you warm congrats.

But If You Like Me…you probably were that same kid, the one with or without a bookbag.

CHAPTER 2

# Wake Up

If You Look Like Me…you were happy with the way you were created. You often questioned if you were doing right or wrong or if you were ever appreciated. Knowing the journey ahead could be risky, dangerous and scary…who to trust, who to look up to, who will guide you, who will take you seriously enough to stand beside you…family? Friends or strangers who lie too?

If You Look Like Me…you probably felt denied as if you weren't worth the truth, but it seems to be a lot easier when you stay true to you…like when you were twenty-one and thought you knew everything…you thought life was going to be handed to you and you'd be kept out of harm's way, just like you had dreamed.

If You Look Like Me…you had moments where you felt powerless, no strength to move forward because there's no "I" in team.

Time waits for no one, and no one waits to leave.

If You Look Like Me…you may have decided to plant your own seed, take on bigger chances, let the past pass you, because there's so much more in the world than greed, while learning about yourself and knowing yourself is all you'll ever need.

If You Look Like Me…you had moments where you felt powerless, no strength to move forward because there's no "I" in team.

Time waits for no one, and no one waits to leave.

If You Look Like Me…you may have decided to plant your own seed, take on bigger chances, let the past pass you, because there's so much more in the world than greed, while learning about yourself and knowing yourself is all you'll ever need.

If You Look Like Me…you dressed a certain way…whether rags, riches or things people gave. Shoes didn't matter, but then hardly anything fits the same. What's better than being a people's person, then you notice how people change.

If You Look Like Me…nothing looks familiar, so you try to look at things in different ways!

CHAPTER 3

# Balance

If You Look Like Me…there is a point in time when not much is worth looking at, the sun rises then falls, and once again you'll feel the need to step back. The world suddenly changes; progression becomes fameless and that life as an adolescent remains nameless.

If You Look Like Me…sometimes it was hard to think…do I follow, lead by example? What's wrong with you? Think! You've pictured yourself being the next big thing…ideas come and go, but nothing syncs. Did you become that? I DON'T KNOW…I guess it depends on what "That" means!

If You Look Like Me…you understood it's not always best to put your best foot forward, but nothing is at its best until it's complete. Nervousness becomes your worst enemy. How? When my only enemy is me? It's just that some things you can't admit to yourself, but admitting is the first step to being free.

If You Look Like Me…you've focused on better things and dreamt bigger dreams. You tried understanding people from a human perspective, not knowing where that leads. What's an animal? What's a being? Am I a mammal? Are they even equal? Why do questions go unanswered? Are we really people?

If You Look Like Me…lots of things fed your ego…you learned how to walk, talk and be a hero. Just like a newborn, everything starts from ground zero!

CHAPTER 4

# Views and Values

If You Look Like Me…you have views and values, different but the same. You like certain temperatures, foods, drinks, smells, touches, sounds and people you may or may not want around.

You make choices you like and dislike, and that's different than being proud. You agree and disagree, some call it debating…but that's how you view life…and sometimes all you can say is "WOW!"

If You Look Like Me…you're not always wrong or right. I mean, you can take a wild guess and still feel like it's just life. There's no truth to differences…some things you've rejected, some things you've accepted.

If You Look Like Me…there's a lot of things you just can't question… with every experience comes a lesson. Will You Get It? I questioned myself at times because at times I needed a few seconds.

If You Look Like Me…nice things becomes a blessing, effort becomes relentless…the seeds you once planted are now growing faster than expected. Who was responsible for you, now them? Weren't you in those same shoes? Or did you not give things life too?

If You Look Like Me…there are certain messages you valued. Like that old saying, "A hard head makes a soft…ha ha ha, okay, I think you know where that leads to. But growing up is not always something we'll go through. We'll make errors, think we're clever and even make excuses for what we didn't do.

If You Look Like Me…trials and tribulations don't stop where you do or want them to if that's what you choose. You can race them, face them or try to replace them…there's always an angle we're not used to. I can say forget it all and turn my back on everything or see it through and not wonder if it ever changed.

If You Look Like Me...you've probably tried and are still thinking the same.

## Chapter 5

# Wellness

IF YOU LOOK LIKE ME …you're probably in good health. Maybe there are some complications, and you've been hard on yourself. The bigger picture is not always as clear as day… most do the unnecessary, but what's necessary is not always the way.

IF YOU LOOK LIKE ME…hardship will make you think twice and play it safe.

Taking risks is never a bad thing, what's bad is not having a plan A.

IF YOU LOOK LIKE ME…tunnel vision is like having a third eye, you see things differently, so there's no need to race. What's simpler than moving at your own pace? What moves you will guide the true you if you allow it to lead the way.

**IF YOU LOOK LIKE ME...** loved one's have a special meaning, like having your own special place. If when you feel the love never comes, you're still one who is loved, and that's a special greeting on any day, just turn and say "hey". Just a simple gesture : Hi, Hello, How Are You ? How is your day....? Keep living, loving and enjoy life.... you'll thank you, more than anyone could ever say.

IF YOU LOOK LIKE ME…everything is okay or maybe you just roll with the punches because it could be worse if you let it eat you away. Don't give up on your beliefs or your dreams, no matter who doesn't agree. Making your own rules is the ultimate tool, and that's an ultimate key, just be safe and unafraid of your own views.

IF YOU LOOK LIKE ME…you've imagined yourself exploring the world in one day…and every state, country and continent knows your face…that's a dream I once had, now my dreams wish I could stay.

IF YOU LOOK LIKE ME…counting stars were like counting sheep, the brighter they get the more your mind leaps, until you fall fast asleep.

Chapter 6

# Your Own Twos

Now that you're on your journey, the roads have become steep, hills turn to mountains, and the wind makes you feel like a leaf.

IF YOU LOOK LIKE ME…that's peace. That are more reasons to move your feet. No looking back on what could've been, 'cause what's wrong in the real world is not always a sin.

IF YOU LOOK LIKE ME…you'll never give in.  A loss is a loss, doesn't mean you'll never win. Smile, grin… hold up your chin, wipe your eyes, wash your face…love the skin you're in. Take pride in your accomplishments, 'cause if you never say never, some doors may never open again.

IF YOU LOOK LIKE ME…you can stand the heat, you've had ups and downs, and you've been weak. You've found your strengths, and you didn't sink, you pulled yourself out of the trenches but yet you still have to reach your peak.

IF YOU LOOK LIKE ME…that feeling will never end. It's just the beginning, and that's how life begins. Those are the things you value…like things you look up to…not many things I valued, because my vision didn't always have a clear view.

**IF YOU LOOK LIKE ME…I** salute you…no, I mean the other you, the one who's a mommy, a daddy, brother, sister, aunt, uncle, cousin, grandma, grandpa, niece, nephew and best friend too!

CHAPTER 7

# The Next Move

IF YOU LOOK LIKE ME…you probably lived in a world and said, "Wow, what a shame" or you're happy with the world you live in and don't want to see change. I, too, was once selfish, stuck in my own ways. Now that I've experienced my experiences, I've had to realize we're all still the same.

IF YOU LOOK LIKE ME... wealth, health, politics and religion are apart of life's game. I felt the world I lived in was just a big ball going down in flames. Sure, every day is a new challenge, but things that happens daily, seem to come in the same lane.

IF YOU LOOK LIKE ME…there's time, then there's a time frame… there's change, then there's a sudden change. I felt confused and amused because I could only adapt to certain things. If you knew better, you'd do better…yeah, I've done better, just never knew I was that clever.

IF YOU LOOK LIKE ME…opportunity was on a whole other level. You do what you have to, or you'll struggle. Overcoming the fear of failure can't be influenced by your peers. You have to look deep within yourself and accept the roads that travel further than the ears.

IF YOU LOOK LIKE ME…the next move has to be the best move, let your eyes see what your mind thinks, and it'll all make sense every time you blink. Relax…you got it from here, keep moving forward…just don't sink!

CHAPTER 8

# Stand Tall

IF YOU LOOK LIKE ME…You've made a pledge to greatness…seeing is believing but even the hardest steps, you have to take them. Be a focused person, remain human and true. Glory and suffering are legacies that made you, you.

IF YOU LOOK LIKE ME…you honour the struggle and respect the success, no matter what you do, strive to bring new life in a world of uncertainty when chaos doesn't rest.

IF YOU LOOK LIKE ME…it's empowering to be loving, sharing and creative…work, study and listen… because we all can use a favor. There's so much to learn and so much we can teach. Self-reliance through resurrection, you'll even hear yourself speak.

IF YOU LOOK LIKE ME…you too, started as a youth, some of us may have had a head start…some may not have had the patience to want to leave their mark. Discipline, courage and devotion…which direction are we going?

A free mind determines self-worth… but so much goes unspoken.

IF YOU LOOK LIKE ME…you've been bent, broke and broken, until there's nothing else holding!

CHAPTER 9

# Take It Easy

IF YOU LOOK LIKE ME…some things won't be easy. Move accordingly at your own speed.

YES! Time runs its own marathon….with you, around you, sometimes even behind you. But there's always time to do what you need to. But getting ahead of yourself can damage things you never mean to, and that's mean too.

IF YOU LOOK LIKE ME…then you've seen the sun rise and fall, yeah….that's life timing you.

Rushing to do nothing because you didn't have a clue, sitting in traffic or just standing and imagining…is this action or am I just overreacting?

IF YOU LOOK LIKE ME…there's more to life than to just live and die…how could I complain about life if I've never tried to feel alive? Then there's the other side, and every story won't seem wise, but that's a story you can't downsize or minimize…take the second chance, just don't live it a third time. Reminds me of many who didn't get it on the first try, then there was me, looking at my own eyes.

IF YOU LOOK LIKE ME…your mind was always dancing, not just to music, but to the most odd sounds, like clapping…and that makes you happy. That makes you want to move forward, you've accomplished something…doesn't matter if you show it.

IF YOU LOOK LIKE ME…the things that aren't going your way may seem boring, no more excitement, no more exploring. Challenging every thought that's keeping your mind from soaring. Like cloudy days with no chance of rain, but it's steadily pouring.

IF YOU LOOK LIKE ME…you tend to be more focused, unaware of the stares like nothing's ever noticed. Even now, during and after matters, just keep going. Pay close attention to how things are approaching…fast, slow and slower motion, it's still in motion…control it!

## Chapter 10

# No Regrets

IF YOU LOOK LIKE ME…accepting your losses and fears can be tricky. Being aware of what could be or what may not happen can make your strengths disappear, faster than you think, just to be clear. Don't go anywhere. You've applied so much heart for so many years. Besides, remembering what's at stake.

IF YOU LOOK LIKE ME…anger makes it easy to stay awake. So much has taken over your mind that it hurts to think. The blind can't lead the blind, but sometimes those who see the signs still can't see straight. What's the point of being sober if it feels the same as having a drink, anyway?

IF YOU LOOK LIKE ME…you are human, a living being. Nothing's wrong with feeling weak. If you don't recognize the enemy, what's there to breach? What makes sense will come to light, no matter if it's wrong or if it right. Just because the world is not nice, still believe some day that everything will be alright. Because its your reality and you've paid the price.

IF YOU LOOK LIKE ME…setting your pride aside is more expensive than cheap. I've made unnecessary sacrifices. If I was any less perfect, I would say I love to gamble, but it's more difficult than rolling a pair of dice. Mistakes are exceptional, when enough is enough…do you still feel it was worth it or just acceptable?

# THE ENDING OF PART ONE

At this moment, I would like to take the time to thank you for reading IF YOU LOOK LIKE ME. I hope you enjoyed it as much as I did writing it.

Writing this book wasn't an easy journey for me, but it has been a delightful experience. I owe it all to you: the readers, audience, family, friends and anyone else who lent me their support…1 am mostly grateful for all you!

THANKS AGAIN,
with Love, Peace and Prosperity!

S.A. POOLE

www.ingramcontent.com/pod-product-compliance
Ingram Content Group UK Ltd.
Pitfield, Milton Keynes, MK11 3LW, UK
UKHW022222230426
12048UKWH00016BA/1004